BEDS IN THE EAST

Beds in the East

JASON ENG HUN LEE

EYEWEAR PUBLISHING

First published in 2019
by Eyewear Publishing Ltd
Suite 333, 19-21 Crawford Street
Marylebone, London WIH IPJ
United Kingdom

Cover design and typeset by Edwin Smet
Author photograph by Aaron T. Michelson
Printed in England by TJ International Ltd, Padstow, Cornwall

The right of Jason Eng Hun Lee to be identified as author of
this work has been asserted in accordance with section 77
of the Copyright, Designs and Patents Act 1988
ISBN 978-1-912477-82-1

WWW.EYEWEARPUBLISHING.COM

for Anna and Jasper,
my very own Team Lee

Born in the UK in 1984,
Jason Eng Hun Lee is a poet of mixed British
and Chinese-Malaysian ancestry. He has been published
and anthologised in the UK, Hong Kong, Singapore, was
nominated for a Pushcart Prize in 2010, and was a finalist for
the Hong Kong University Prize (2010) and runner-up for the
Melita Hume Prize (2012). A regular contributor to the
Hong Kong literary scene, he holds a PhD in English
Literature and teaches at Hong Kong Baptist University.
This is his debut collection.

TABLE OF CONTENTS

I BEDS IN THE EAST

II THE EDGE OF VAST SHORES

BEDS IN THE EAST

The beds i' the east are soft, and thanks to you
That called me timelier than my purpose hither;
For I have gain'd by 't.

— William Shakespeare,
Antony and Cleopatra

'East? They wouldn't know the bloody East if they saw
it. Not if you was to hand it to them on a plate would
they know it was the East. That's where the East is,
there.' He waved his hand wildly into the black night.

— Anthony Burgess,
The Long Day Wanes: A Malayan Trilogy

OUT OF CHINA

A mother boards a wooden skiff,
swings one son over the edge
then another, and again another

until five boys stand among meagre stores,
each one a weighty sack
contemplating his own heavy load.

And as they push off from shore
one son, my grandfather, will grab
a fistful of pebbles to test his strength,

his white knuckles will ripple with the waves
as my clenched hand underwrites
their exodus in the spirals of this pen.

Amid sails that toss and fly like torn paper
I too will cross these unknown straits
and be cast into the sea's rough cradle,

will stoop across this deck and feel
a straining vessel founder upon reefs
as sharp as any anguished, rallying cry.

This will be our first voyage together,
and should our spirits falter in the dusk
as the wind dies down, as though becalmed,

we'll set our lamps down in the dark
and steady our craft through restless hands.
Those faint grey lines will find their shape,

as we anchor our memory off a new landscape.

BEDS IN THE EAST

Curiosity buzzed by on flimsy dragonfly wings
to take a child through his first prodigal flight,
lifting him across shrieking floorboards, gangly porches,
past scalding words, to pry outside among the world.

There, the streets jostled for space to spread welcome sights.
A blue shawl pressed its velvet light across a fence and smiled,
idling by rows of whitewashed houses that winked and crowned
the inhabitants. Abdul, Rashid, Lim, de Souza.

Bicycles vaulted over potholes, swerved through split papaya.
An old man lugged his wares down the road
keeping the dawn hours with his pealing cry – *telur, telur,*
his wheelbarrow of eggs hissing and popping from crates.

As the muezzin raised his voice over minarets, a mynah bird
recited its sweet, faithful call back over the hill.
The *masjid* reared its golden dome in wonder
while unbelievers sought out its high-pitched sound.

Such days switched on rains that irked then slushed,
a cold rusty sound, to send kids out with mugs and tin cups.
The drains pattered and gushed aloud their complaint
but the streams, willed on by the children, kept flowing.

This is how it opens up for me, the strains of another life,
the land spread beneath me like a magic carpet,
a mother who pointed and said, child, do not be afraid,
who picked me up and showed me, curled up in her arms,

the quayside rolling westward in the beckoning surf,
the sea gypsies roaming by on waves, invincible,
the quiet streets naming one by one the world's children
and a lone dragonfly, euphoric, rising with the morning sun.

LION DANCE

Discarded, it lay brooding in its chest
until that day came when we raced like cubs,
my sister and I, to see who would claim
its swollen head and who would shake the tail
with their squat behind as we mauled the tiles
and lunged across roads in full attire.

While one headed the crest of a black wave
the other furnished the ripple and beat
a silent drum, *de dum de dum dum dum*,
left foot kicked out as the right circled in,
hips heaving under the raging cotton
while dad held the lettuce within arm-shot.

Its goggle-eyed trance brought us red packets
by porches as we sought magical ends
in our private concert, bells jangling in
our challenging ears as we pulled the strings
and fought visitors swirling in red mist
while the gongs resounded and cymbals clashed.

All week we toiled our self-made myths on streets
parading the worn cloth under the sun,
but after the celebrations, the lion
slunk back into its accustomed darkness,
its custodianship lost on us, who were
unfit to stop its spirit from dying out.

CATCHING GRASSHOPPERS

We took turns out in the long grass,
knee-deep in sweat-stained inspiration,
stroking the garden for grasshoppers.
That first one came leaping out,
kneading its legs and skimming through
the humid air like a jet spring.
When of a sudden it landed we shuttered
that spot with anything we could find –
lunch boxes, oversized caps, even once
my palms substituted for a dark green prison.
The light throbbing leapt once, twice,
then dug into quiet protest, waiting
for my sleight of hand to flood day into night.

We kept them in round plastic boxes
fringed with memories of yesterday's catch,
and counted clockwise from the largest,
burliest male with its antennae erect like antlers,
bulbous eyes warming in the transparent gloom.
We tilted the box and saw up close their mandibles
clicking for revenge, breathing tightly
with their hind legs poised for momentum.
That month we culled the grasshoppers every way,
stabbed them with forks and toasted them
over the brown grass, drowned them in pairs
under the reflected glare of sunlight, and fed them
to praying mantis at the stroke of noon.

Then I remember how, tanning after the sun,
the child in me sought solace in their placid ways.
Sounds like the scraping of nature against metal
inside the box enforced a common stand

as I strode against the shrieks of classmates
and scattered them like grains against the wind.
The grasshoppers whined through the air,
like schoolboys at play, and their joy
fanned over the field so swiftly I felt,
for a brief second, I had flown with them,
into the freshness of another world.

RAFFLESIA

I stuttered through each syllable that spiked
and bloomed from the undergrowth of my tongue
and cleared the space around it. Ra-*flesh*-a.
Books told me it was the largest flower,
but I saw through its disguise, sucking up
the moist air and gurgling its threats to me,
spurting out its effluvia onto vines
that ran across feet, rising as fungi.

Folk warned me not to stray too far from paths
where it lay dormant, steaming and rotting.
Its pock-marked leather hide hunched itself up
in a flurry of stench and carrion,
waiting to draw some curious child in
with its rimmed mouth, beckoning me to peer
close like a fly into its tucked up folds.

Yearly we wound through mountainside and parks
while I recalled my list of brutish plants:
the pitcher with its swelling gourd, gorging
on its prey like a fat bellied schoolkid,
the spider orchids dangling red feelers
over my unguarded back, but always
it was Rafflesia I feared most of all.

That day I swore I'd approach the clearing
and inform the crowd of its violent ways,
but when I came upon its charred black bud,
curled up as though fried and lynched by the sun,
I weighed up my distaste for that crude plant
and saw past its fitful aberration,
thinking, within this jungle's primal law,
it was all a question of survival.

PET TERROR

Swaddled up to the neck in murky depths,
face poked out like a mock schoolteacher,
this pet terror showed no fun
relocated in his new surroundings,
stared at by boys on wooden stools,
an outcast glaring back through
gauzy lidless eyes while
storing hostile images of himself.

My classroom was his garden though
this veteran retired from moral fables long ago.
His taste for blood unnerved even me,
waiting to ensnare the next hand
that came within striking distance.
Squat, huddled on his own rancour,
a mine imploding of its own free will.

His crusted shell grew thicker each day
while his upturned bowl stored the sulk
and dregs of his bitter medicine.
He was stuck in a rut and proud of it,
his ignoble grudge outlasting itself,
arched brows craning above the heat,
limbs dangling from the home he'd never know,
the comfort he would never seek.

How he stored such stiffness in his bones,
how he carried it awkwardly
like a heavily laden backpack to school.
Even then I wanted to know
when he would slough off his own back
and leave it all behind him,
slink through the gates
and make his quick getaway.

THE CHAMELEON

Not hunter but prey sought out
from these bushes. Star performer
in this game of hide and seek.
As the slow day counts its hours,
the predator lends his claws speed
and the rest scatter for the trees.

Where the grass ends the race begins.
Reptilian eyes dart from corners
as bulkier forces hunker on the surface,
peer boss-eyed at foliage in front,
their gaze trained on any movement
they see blurring in the green.

But this one flexes his short limbs
and shuffles his skin only
to bask in a welcome sun,
sinks down through the undergrowth
and edges forward to stick a tongue
out at the habitual passer-by.

He need not hear the others haul
their sweaty flanks upright and stumble
through the brittle fields with blood
rampaging from ear to ear.
The quick-heeled and the flighty
are caught together in an instant.

He feels the vibrations on the ground,
senses the right moment to skitter
across the clearing, squirm home and call
the languorous sods after their game,
just as the sun reasserts itself
and the newly-hunted rush off again.

WHITE WOMAN

THE CHAMELEON

Or, as we whispered round corners
behind her back, *Orang Putih*,
giggling incessantly and tracking
her through markets, concealed
in our slacks and slippers, while she,
more modestly clad, rustled by.

Folk greeted her with curved smiles
while kids fumbled arms beside her,
shocked at the contrast of her colour.
The coolie boys baulked and stared
at their tawny skin, pubescent sweat
tanning them daily in the heat.

The Malay women cooed their rhythm,
missee, you buy, you buy, holding up
lush mangosteen, rambutan, in full
outstretched hands, pleading smiles,
only to thumb proudly at her back,
ya, orang putih come buy from me.

Once, falling over myself I gored
my own knee open and there she was,
a crisp white hankie ready to daub
the shame from all those anxious looks.
I froze as she cupped my face with soft palms.
Reluctant, staring up at mother's face.

AUNTIE AGNES

She came singing the Filipino Blues
and adorning crosses in our old room,
holding out her basket of love to swell
our sallow cheeks with her nourishing food.
We aspired to be subs for her kids,
our counterparts leapt at us across seas
but fell short, drowned out by jealous laughter
and the jury of photos by her side.

Once, we had rats paddling across floorboards.
Eyes, like pale moons, peered at us through blankets
so we ran past corridors after her,
ducking rules and confinements to surface
at her warm side, wide-eyed and fearful, not
relenting until she snuffed them with bait,
flung a cleaver through their necks and put us
back to bed, drawing blinds across foreheads.

We took her to our hearts, bought her bangles
and begged for her to come with us on trips.
At the pier, she nodded at mum and waved
us away as we pulled faces. But then,
we returned that month to a vacant room,
the window jailed shut, the bed made, no creak
of doors, no sign of her, our selfless maid
betrayed, cast off by our possessive love.

FAMILY GATHERING

We met one morning at the big Blue House
where bright parcels stacked on veranda boards
hinted at a picnic, but when we wound
through the coarse white sand towards the long grass,
I heard the reeds of ancestral whispers
streaming in my ears, and knew this outing
would summon the full and reverent awe
of grandparents I'd never met before.

Together, they lay reclined on headstones,
their portraits held up in meditation
as someone mopped dew from grandpa's forehead
and swept the undergrowth from his wild feet.
Next, the plinth raised itself to a table,
the mood was lit up by thick incense sticks,
sheets were spread and chopsticks proffered upright
in bowls of rice accompanied by wine.

Opaque, unassuming, they reflected
their gratitude but kept stony silent
as the tinted foil opened to reveal
suckling pig, oranges and sweet pastries.
Though hungry, I kept both hands in pockets
as Eldest Uncle bowed and served them first,
but still I was dragged before them, guilty,
my father's grizzly hand on my shoulder.

One cousin suggested we fly kites but
I admonished him – 'be nice to Ah Kong'.
I was on my best behaviour that day
and gingerly set everything aflame;
the money burned quickly under my stare

but I would not let up, knowing each night
my grandparents would perch themselves on walls
and keep their vacant eyes trained upon me.

TURTLE ISLAND

A fine turquoise ocean rolled over me
while I spluttered and sank like a blunt stone,
imitating the turtle's slow descent.
The white froth and tang had elected me
its guardian, prying among seaweed, quartz
and shell fragments for signs of its cluster.

Closer to land and the palm stalks glistened
in the raw heat, heavy with excitement
as I mapped the sand dunes, turning over
troughs of white ash in my hand, keeping track
of those speckled eggs, incubating lies
in the battened hatch of my sand-filled brain,

treading carefully, fearful for the sound
of cracked shells, of carapaces oozing
in their green sludge, steering clear of the shoals
and the restless surge of foam churning up
more salt-offensive seaweed, sea urchins
and other claws that would latch onto me.

That night, we quarrelled round the naked lamp
and peered silently at the first dark swell.
Waves picked their feet as the first she-turtle
tossed her head and flopped on the sandy plain,
flailing her flipper for help though no one
dared fumble out across the ranger's glare.

Soon she had found her own purchase and we
cheered and formed a procession after her,
watching her unload her spoor of bright eggs,
drawing deep breaths as she filled the hole up

and padded the nest for comfort. Grievous,
her habits done, she wobbled back to sea,

her burden passed to us, accomplices
in the tough love of unborn children,
huddled round the spot like treasure seekers.
My head swam as someone licked their parched lips,
terrified – knowing we weren't the only ones
who thought they were worth their weight in gold.

SCHOOL PARADE

In the *padang*, morning sweat glistening
on our brows, eyes squinting devilishly
at our national sun, we sang our hearts
out of tune as the flags rose solemnly
above our heads to clutter up the skies.

First the national, state, then school anthem,
all blurred into one long song which tapered
off with the principal's sonorous drone
as monitors leered at us from the back
and mosquitoes tagged us on the rank fields.

Throughout August we learned of *Merdeka*,
how the British were fought and overthrown
by all our patriotic forefathers –
I too yelled death to the invaders then
bit my tongue for fear of home reprisals.

I wanted to fly kites, or thrash marbles,
but as the celebrations gathered storm
there was no let up. Shirts were inspected,
shoes acquired spit and we scuffled round
the field, chained together in one labour.

Such songs I would never forget, such pomp,
the way trumpets blundered through untrained ears,
our heads chasing madness, each with eyes fixed
on the distance, conspiring to evade
service to school and its oppressive rule.

THE KERIS SPEAKS

I come bathed in fire
and metal from distant meteors.
My antiquarian roots will hold me
in place to carve my history
in wood or ivory, sustain
me with enamel
and dark lacquer.
I will take shape
in the broad base
of this hilt that
guards and supports me, winding through me like
molten wedge or silver, folded over and over,
my intricate pattern etched in nickel and iron,
my colour and identity. I will undulate
like *naga* in his dance of death
as my sinuous body slides
softly beneath a pillow.
The blood of a father
and his father runs in
my black ornate veins
and I will inherit his son,
kiss his forehead and feed
him with love and venom.
You too can be my master.
Call me and I will stand on
end and do all that you bid.
I will ward off fire and fate
to protect and honour you.
You must know where you
stand when you wield me,
hold me aloft and bathe
me in lime and incense,

and never cross me
for I cut both ways.
I will rattle in my
sheath, run amok
in the crowd, your
every command
on the tip of my
tongue. Just
say the word.
Go on.
Say
it.

SHADOW THEATRE

The late night procession rings in,
the farmers stow away their hoes,
beneath the glow of an oil lamp
a hush falls on the village rows,
but once the elders assemble
their impatient voices tremble:

Play the Wayang for us, Tok Dalang,
the deeds of Rama, Sita, Hanuman,
play your chorus upon the gamelan
whose resonant hums have now begun.

Behind the cloth, ancestral foes
align themselves upon a stage,
from slender parchments their spirits
echo scenes from a bygone age.
Good and evil, their final stand,
awoken by tremulous hands:

Sing the Wayang for us, Tok Dalang,
the words that Krishna spoke to Arjuna,
sing verses of the Mahabharata
from whose ancient tongue our myths have sprung.

Poet-playwright, the *Dalang* moves
and the throes of battle resume.
With mouths spread and arms aquiver
the light ushers upon the gloom.
Now music soothes his final cue
as shadow puppets slide from view:

End the Wayang for us, Tok Dalang,
the tales of all our Dewas and Vedas,
end the night's long vigil against the sun
for dawn has come. Our work must be done.

THE LONGHOUSE

Between misty cloud and sea,
under the care of *Aki Nabalu*,
ancestor mountain,

the longhouse reclines upon its stools
and basks in the lie of its land,
observing the harvest as an old man.

Running fingers along its grooved back,
slats creaking under wizened bark,
it loosens the vines around its trunk

to expand its knotted roots again,
as yet another family comes to spread
their bounty beneath its ageing fronds.

More hands to pound grain in the storehouse
and sweep across the long corridor.
It remembers once how,

a young strapling out amongst fields,
it dreamt of *Huminodun* and her sacrifice,
saw a girl's reflection in the brooks

and thought, she will be my harvest queen!
She will grasp the *padi* stalks under my possessive shade
and soothe me at night with her lullabies.

Now its thatched roof swells, ruffles with the wind
as if to say, come, sit here
and breathe through my wooden palms,

inhale the smoky reeds
and feast on *tapai* with me;
listen to the pipes and drums falling –

forget the plantations, the veins
of white sap and gold,
dance to the rich seam of my forebears,

this is the life you have come for.
Though others will stumble through
these muddy fields, you will never leave.

KINABATANGAN

Deeper and deeper, they meandered down the river,
through oxbow lakes, slicing through
the brown sludge, picking up mud and silt
as they coursed along in rickety barges.

Seafarers from another land,
they jostled for position on the river's shoulder,
driving through hinterland that would pull
them in but later call itself theirs.

A coarse rustling in trees nearby made them
aware of their own presence, a conspicuous
murmur of vines – the knowledge that
someone else had been there before.

Porcelain jars, lacquerwork
and ceramics laboured in the damp hold,
offsetting the wares they would be exchanged for:
beeswax, rattan, precious resin, bounty of the forest.

They were on the lookout for bird nests,
the flimsy woven spit that hardened into diamonds,
held in a giant cleft of hill or rocky outcrop
that sprang to life in a cauldron of bats.

Fears moistened. The surrounding plains
could muster an uprising, upset their course
and flood the river's bank. Crocodiles, aroused
by ripples in the mangrove, thrashed in their mating.

Hours later, the canopy slipped off its vegetation
and announced a clearing – an abandoned outpost.

Or was it razed in a feud? Night descended on them,
swapping crestfallen looks with a burnt patch of earth.

Having come all the way in, there would be
no turning back. The current yielded no progress,
the water stilled and lapped the bank softly,
levelling its mud flat against the stranded boat.

No choice now but to alight and set up store.
Even the ground stood firm against their intrusion
as fireflies switched their torches on in the gloom
and the hornbill's bright dagger beckoned from afar.

SONS OF THE SOIL

Cruising along miles of empty road,
we watch the jungle reel back and give way
to lines of oil palm on either side,
their fronds swaying in unison.

These were the plantations, the state's
new frontier, untapped hinterland
hewn out of woods and rising
up new checkpoints and villages.

As we slow past one *kampung*
I glimpse from dusty panes at lean figures
raking their steely teeth across ground
hard as any in the cracks of morning.

Their shadows overgrown by giant billboards,
scraping no living from their hoes,
the land is fertilised only by upstart
memories of their solitary toil.

I imagine their backs breaking
over blood-sapping rubber trees,
their pain chiselled onto hunched features
and muscles dripping with golden sweat.

Though we all held out for similar claims,
surely they were children of the soil;
theirs was the noblest, most ignominious
act of abasement to their motherland.

But the peninsula had hemmed them in,
promised much and given little in return.

Legislation had signed them off while bushfires
kept them confined in its yellow haze.

Cultivating their ties each day,
forced to subsist on such effrontery,
what deeds or earth-born titles have they received,
these *bumiputera* friends of mine?

ACCIDENT

From across the street there came a strange wail,
a bold ululating sound that roused prayers
and shouts of *ambulans*! *Cepat*! And though
no one could have foreseen the act, there was
an instinct that made our shock culpable,
a sense we should have known better perhaps.

There was a gathering in streets as mum
held us tightly, while different accents
answered a register with fists and sobs.
A girl turned and asked where big brother was,
yet only when it appeared in papers
did it acquire monumental status.

A dozen photos stared out from the page
while splayed below them like a hunter's catch
was the carcass of a bus, short of breath,
its orange paintwork twisted, flecked with grey,
never to squat intently on corners
or part its jaws for reluctant school kids.

United in their grief, some made the trek
a mile or so downhill to lay bouquets
and water their anguish in blooming sobs.
Given to routine, others slowed beside
the post that kept its head bowed in remorse
before it was replaced with a bright sign.

It comes back to me, that year's unspoken
eulogy, tracking the first taint of death,
its faint whirring echo beyond the fan.
My palms hastened their way through taught prayers,
peeling the damp pages back as the ink
ran through, illegible, like my first tears.

BEDTIME STORY

after Ralph McTell

Nightly, when the muezzin descended
his tower of faith and the day's lesson
flashed a final time to the rhythm of
a teacher's cane, I snuggled into bed
with my old picture book of London
and found its mighty embankment
soaring past my tropical reverie.

The white mist of page descended onto the streets
with their marble promises and solemn colonnades,
flat faces in curled up smiles and bowler hats
doffed one to the other – 'after you, sir',
'no, I insist, after you' – textured garments
felt through curious fingertips.

Page after page thickly smudged with lines
of warm pastel, each shade evoked a
child's instinct for signs.
Red for postage, red for buses,
red for the bustle and swagger of the guards,
black for the velvet curtains drawn across evenings
in the theatre of my head.

What I sought most between the covers
was the golden end to a bed-time story,
the promise of a reawakened land,
skipping through the pavements with
a pound chewing through my pocket.

But on that final corner I bumped into an old woman
who stared at me through my reverie and said:
let me take you by the hand
and lead you through the streets of London,
I'll show you something
to make you change your mind.

PASSION FRUIT TREE

As mango and papaya fruit were out of reach
I found my newly-planted passion fruit tree,
seeded fresh from the ripeness of my brain,
the sweetest and best companion of my childhood.

I nourished it daily, lavished rain on its bed,
massaged the soil beneath to find cause for its shyness
when for the first month my green relation
would not show its vivid colours.

Compared to my neighbour's groves
of well-disciplined trees, my only charge
festered and skulked in shade against the fence,
afraid of its exposure to the midday sun.

I poured my lore and compassion
into that disabled stranger, my vigilance
bearing no fruit as I kept invading the water tank
for some elixir to soothe its blistering knees.

Those infant periods led me to new corners
of my world as I scouted ahead in my sleep
to see how both our gnarled limbs
would clasp at life at the edges.

For a time I had a run with its habits;
some seizure overtook its shyness
and it gushed, alive with the fullness of its birth
to throw its vines against the breeze.

Then some distant call like an old nursery song
came wafting in as a message of the times.
A door opened and told me we were moving
and my imagination struck up a fire that devoured that tree.

THE EDGE
OF VAST SHORES

I am but a small child wandering upon the
vast shores of knowledge, every now and then finding a
small bright pebble to content myself with...

– Plato

And this gray spirit yearning in desire
To follow knowledge like a sinking star,
Beyond the utmost bound of human thought.

– Lord Alfred Tennyson, 'Ulysses'

BECOMING

What the eyes can see, the hands cannot hold.
Your heart's compass whirls around and won't stand still.
It sets itself at rest beyond the sunset,
past flights that set no bounds, have no stable home.
This is where the present flows.
This is my becoming.

Learn to mutate the land, its blurred contours.
Sweep the heart's passage across the darkness.
I have learnt to trust my own judgement,
trust the shortcomings of time.
This is no loss of control.
This is just becoming.

Find the old stars fading in the sky,
strip the old symbols from all the new signs.
Loosen thoughts from things divine:
nothing finds itself in place for long.
This is how the world revolves.
This is life becoming.

TERRA INCOGNITA

Abroad in England, we pitched
our first home like a winter camp,
pulled on old fleeces and furs,
stopped up bottles, unwound bedrolls,

supplied ourselves in the long forage,
the endless torrents of snow,
planning our grand campaign
into the great unknown.

So 'here be dragons' I say,
billowing my breath into smoke,
obscuring distance for miles around,
seeing no further than my nose.

The markers are deceptive here:
balancing the map upside-down,
I abandon old assumptions
regarding omens and intuition.

Night envelops quickly, its weight
hangs over this northern sky,
and for every star that blinks
an unfamiliar light is switched on.

The rime-covered firs, the lakes
coated in a slurry of ice,
the gently rounded slopes and sleds
that shattered mirrors on the earth,

all these would prove conquerable.
My soul may find a resting place here,
a plateau or cairn of crystal to prove
some first markings on this land.

So let me plant my soles firm in this tundra
and set the flag on this hostile terrain,
claim some satisfaction
from this first of winter trips,

my sudden footfalls as hallowed
as a snow-paddler trespassing
nature's unknown straits.
My driving race towards its pole.

QUARRY HILL

That steep hill I peered down at
from school fed on its own myth,
so named because the town once
housed a Victorian chalk pit,
with this school as dumping ground
as I was led to believe then,
when snot-nosed mornings streamed
from their long corridors and
marked me out as the foreign
object for the students' quarry.

Chalked white from past industry,
it smelt faintly of burnt custard,
a filling-station for the bric-a-brac
memories no one else wanted.
And yet I was fascinated,
those smooth-freighted landscapes
fenced off from everyday existence,
the hoardings rusted and broken
like a lost little wasteland where
I would read other people's childhood.

At school, those board marker lines
outlined the territory of rough kids,
some hierarchy I could follow
yet never understand, and though
I knew the playground games
with their intricate nonsense rhymes,
I enjoyed most the race to the pit.
For unlike them, I wanted to excavate
my own being, dig deeper and find
treasure in the debris of someone else's past.

OLD PHOTOS

Here, stacked up inside the folds of this trunk,
these were the real skeletons of your past.
I fingered them as I would a saint's bones,
a dusty reliquary turned holy
in my hands. Its clinical stench of film
unhinged itself slowly to open up
an assortment of still life images.
You at fifteen, your fresh perm erupting
at the sight of this Oriental man.
His bright specs, mullet and custom-made flares
that dragged you half-way across the dancefloor.

How odd you must have looked to each other.
In a library of opportunity,
I imagine your first demure contact
after school. That and an exchange of notes.
The nine of you squashed into a Mini.
The journey full of his cologne. Southend.
Your two lives unprepared for that long ride.
At times you looked jaded, starved, not hungry
at all. Something had you blocked up. But then
a heavy switch and a sudden darkness
in his room clinched it for you. His last date.

Those church bells tolled before your twentieth.
A short honeymoon at the London Zoo

with your ring finger pecked at by penguins.
The loveshack neither of you could afford.
All that, and your grand adventure abroad,
playing *tai tai* to a new round of friends.
Your inner sanctum swelled with their laughter
but gave no sign of us away in photos.

The camera hid us with father and locked
you into its memory. Only your lovely
eyes stared us back into our existence.

TWO OCARINAS

The ocarinas you bought us stood there,
an unlikely pairing forced
into an unholy communion.
You sat still pursing one to your lips
while I fidgeted to join you in song
and defiled mine with black onerous notes,
fingering its gleaming cavity
and hushing its yelping cries,
my bumbling bass next to your frenzied whine.

Like a bird caged
in its sickly white eggshell,
mine rattled in my hands, shrill,
gasping out puffs of hollow air.
I carried it with me everywhere,
my junior brethren, your heavy watchman
draped round my neck like a chain,
tugging at my lapel, its enamelled form
jealously swaying in close conversation.

After a while, after what felt like years
the pitches came to resemble one,
a symphony of ocarina
that welded in waves the right sounds,
two mellifluous gourds cracking open
in sweet satisfaction as we wet our lips,
our saliva boring through the holes,
but we moved on within ourselves
too haughty to pine on ocarina.

Once abandoned, I return to it now,
clearing out the dust and cobwebs,
ready to savour its jerky song,
its plosive lurch into life,
and that long first faithful act
of two lovers in procession,
in the midst of their first contact.

45 BELGRAVE SQUARE

We waited under the buzz of a rotating fan,
sheets neatly printed against palms,
waiting for my annual summons to citizenship.
Dad led the way, preceding me by thirty years' toil
under a hot tropical sun as we sat under
the crescent gaze of a woman with sharp brows
and a glorious headscarf striped across her forehead.
Passports were handed back awaiting stamps
of approval and the tentative claim
to become native again lasted well into the day.

Flicking through serried pages of childhood exploits
with no visible history, she looked deep beneath
my skin and seethed. 'You don't have the right stamp.'
Round eyes met almond eyes and the pegs didn't fit,
which meant I was an illegal in England unless
'you have a British passport', she glowered,
blue and white asterisks overlapping her blood-shot eyes.
Despite our heavy protests my rights
to Malaysia were revoked and I became alien
to this colonial enclave in an ex-colonial Empire.

Under the whirring fan, I saw my childhood
sucked out of this dual existence,
leaving me dry from the orange tipped sunsets
that tasted of innocence and the luscious peel
of mango that shrivelled up like a disused tongue.
A fruit sagging by the lull of evening.
Attendant now in my own country,
I retraced my way back into a realm inherited
by English hordes and partisans bereft
of nationhood and servility.

As we limped down Trafalgar a sudden shadow
threw its full length across my path.
Nelson himself stood proud across my brow,
signalling do-or-die invites and hailing his
newest recruit to hoist the colours.
Some familiar line from an old textbook
gripped me as he flashed a crooked grin,
the lesson of an age struck from me long ago:
how 'England expects every man to do his duty',
how truly mankind is press-ganged into service.

ISLANDS

But now I only hear
Its melancholy, long, withdrawing roar,
Retreating to the breath
Of the night-wind, down the vast edges drear
And naked shingles of the world.
– Matthew Arnold, 'Dover Beach'

Standing at the edge of vast shores
I hear ancestor spirits
invoke their unbidden siren call

so the sea bursts as they command
the clap of waves that run
between the current and the tide's fall

and 'home, home' come their lilting cries
as their foamy voices roll
over the aspirating surf.

Their arcane faces contort in my mind
and whisper for me to beach myself
on immense rocks that rise nearby

as 'home, home' their booming sighs
reverberate against cliffs,
breaking in tandem, uprearing ties.

52

The sand begins to clutch my feet
and sink back through the eddying swirl
but as my blood lies, constricted in this swell

I pick up a stone, cold as my thoughts
and skim the murmuring waters across –
as the exile in me replies:

I see forebears thrashing horizons near
and wide
to yoke the seas' great churning tides.

I greet them daily beneath chequered skies,
bid them goodnight in a foreign tongue
and rebound the ocean's sigh.

I see mother and father sunder worlds before me
compressing time and space,
compressing culture, compressing me.

But my progeny will be distilled
in different blood from pressing bodies.
They too will come upon this shore.

Roiling in the sands of time
they will find their own skin
rubbing off birth marks.

They too will resist the lull of rocks
and rise up from the ocean's womb,
standing on the edge of something new.

SHIPWRECKED

When you did not return to me that night
I knew that I would find you perched up here,
resting upon the prow of this shipwreck,
peering out across its bleak vantage point
and thinking back on all the days we shared.

Long after we met you came across it,
some merchantman's venture ground to a halt.
Raw nerves had eaten out its famished hull,
dry rot had crept over the wood to form
blots of sepia rust on it, weals of blood.

Like thick, unkempt hair, it smelt of damp hemp
though the deck was smooth and watertight once.
The caulk and tar had peeled back their layers
to show tears seeping through wrinkled boards, as
the tang of salt words sloshed around your mouth.

Grief made you see things as they really were:
the bowsprit slew you like a giant lance,
the wheel's crucifix hung lopsided to
signal that faith had faltered from its course,
leaving the ribs of your ship raw, exposed.

You found no ballast to steady yourself
in me, knowing the ship carried my name.
The tide promised more driftwood, more hard rock
and shingle pounding under your stern as
you stood rudderless at the sea's frontier.

You wanted me to show you a new world,
seeing far out from that mangled shore, lights,
always lights dispersing the mist for you,
praying that I would find your wretched hulk,
fix you up and put you back out to sea.

WHEN SHE LEFT HIM

When she left him he packed up all his books
and hunkered down in his room with rations
taken sparingly each day, never looked
past windows until, after a fashion,
light found no sanctuary in his eyes
and his lips creased up into one last smile.

His stubble grew into a woollen beard
and his limbs turned sullen inside their sleeves,
then things started to crawl into his head
and his chair rocked back and forth in its grief,
and soon the walls grew out from the kitchen
emboldened by his stubborn decision.

Soon the lines were cut, and his phone went dead,
and when cars pulled up and the family peered
through the keyhole there was no slow movement
of doors, no gruff rebuke as they had feared
so when the brigade came with their axes
they rushed the door in a blaze of hatchets.

And his wife, who was a doctor too, came
and bent over to inspect his still frame.
She noted his pulse had lapsed and his skull
had crumpled from a heavy weight. She mulled
the last time light had graced his gnarly skin.
As though something had sucked the life from him.

IN YOUR ABSENCE

I said when you moved into my life,
'fill the room and the room will be yours',
so you took possession of everything
and set them to darkness in your absence.

They will not forget your subtle grace:
the sofa stoops to pick up your weight,
the jar shows you its well of desire, even
the letters spread and fly from memory.

Would that you had not been kind to them,
that you had simply glanced at each object,
not turning your hands over each thing,
filled every cushion with a heart of feathers,

made every cord a connection, switched
the lights on from each remote location.
Tell me then this was not your parting gift,
that you had not joined with their reflections.

Now they pine for you, they clamour as I do
for your presence, your figure walking
through each door, each sudden precipice,
each numb footstep burning in the dark,

so cold to the touch, so absent in spirit.
So full of the love you invested here.
They move only to the command
of the dark shadow you leave behind.

LEEDS, 2003

It all came to me during my first year,
the girls poised and pretty in their dresses,
the rugby boys prowling the corridors,
all summer exchanges yet to begin
against white-washed rosters propped up on walls,
under dim lights behind closed union doors.

And after those sheltered halls, what came next?
The drama of real life. Footballer's wives,
televised speeches and sexed-up reports.
Some gravelly voice hard on civil strife.
And on campus, scrawled in white chalk, someone
would recall the time with these kerbside lines:

Eat Beaver, Save a Tree.
Eat Bush, Save the World.

So much for decency and decorum.
Seduced by this strange body politic,
I must rouse myself up to such studies,
reach out and touch those things untaught to me,
my feigned innocence too late to be saved.
My own wild incursions as yet unmade.

THE WAKE

Already they are drunk in the garden,
the men toying with their drinks, trying
to forget that one amongst them has died,
flipped the switch and hauled bloody heaven down
to prick their guilt and fire their conscience.
The wives usher them by in their small groups
as the children gargle their cries and hurl
onto ashen pavements, so that soon
the more than mere grief is wiped from faces
as the day chokes upon its charred remains.

This is how life goes on, enduring
the hard furnace with bone-raw resistance
while the ashes tip out from fag ends
and billow like smoke toward some unkept world;
the old couples huddled close from habit,
the smiles sunk from brief mutterings on fate,
the air thick with remembrance, as pulses
quicken and normal life storms to its end.

Somewhere, sometime soon, each of them will break
their resolve to scatter home in their wake
and shake to the unknown, hoping against hope,
praying no fire would summon them forth
or call them back to the earth from whence they came,
rising disturbed with each dawn's undertaking,
writhing like the fresh soil that's piled on their graves.

THREE LIONS PUB

And lined along the bar the faithful stood
cradling their beers, their last supper over,
exchanging nerves as before a battle.
The curtains and livery all shone white
with the purity of new religion,
clinical, bedecked with staunch red crosses.
This was more important than life and death,
someone cried. *Did they practice penalties?*
Best chance for a semi-final in years.
The odds were high. Football was coming home.

Already the old mantras were in use,
those coarse slurs as the players emerged to
a chorus of drunken anthems and boos,
shouts of *God wills it, no surrender,*
something about world wars and a world cup.
Lost amidst the crowd, I'm sure I saw
the lout and hipster booming out one voice
in delirium, and I too thought, 'on, on
you noblest English,' trailing fantasies
of camaraderie, esprit de corps.

Yet soon enough the echoing cheers drowned
in the malaise of England's poor start, jeers
resounding this disjointed team of parts,
then whispers from corners, an abyss of staring,
as though eyes stalked the flock for a scapegoat,
and no sooner had the first foul been drawn
one bold figure had charged up to me
to show some offence had been driven home.
You dirty chink, he sneered, then *cheatin scum.*
You fuckers should go back home to China.

Tensions spiked. The match was well underway
but from somewhere another scoreline read out
in the faces of those gathered round.
Somewhere, the smothered pride of an island
had roused its full pot-bellied rage, pumping
its fists at me, baiting me into words.
'Listen mate, I'm just here to watch the match.'
I don't care if yer sellin dodgy gear,
cheap DVDs, you cunts ain't welcome ere.
En-ger-land. That's where this fuckin place is.

The counter leant against me. I was trapped
in six yards of space, bereft of support,
braced for conflict until these words rang out:
Oi. Leave im alone. He ain't done nothing!
Yeah, pick on someone yer own size. Sniggers.
Ain't his fault they come here for a free ride.
Of course, I forgot how the English loved
to lend their support to an underdog.
Free kicks were taken, insults were traded
and my own team now formed up around me.

The first lot had pints in hand, arms akimbo,
glazed foreheads, tattoos and militant eyes;
the supporting crowd, younger, numerous,
waved colourful alcopops and cocktails.
Hey. Why are you siding with him? These cunts
take all our jobs, our benefits, our homes,
it's like a fuckin government hand-out.
He raised his arms like a priest giving alms,
his sanctimonious act drawing shouts of
hear hear and *fuckin right* and *ere we go.*

Just then the screen flickered – England had scored.
The belligerents dropped their litany
of filth and joined in the celebrations,
tumbling chairs, shattering glass, spilling beer.
Yeah, have sum of that you cunts. Engerland.
When the fuss had died down eyes turned to me
again, emboldened by the lead they shared
and pressing on with their home advantage.
Oi, chink, don't think you're gettin off the hook,
that first skinhead said, spurting more bile at me.

So once more the old epithets raged forth,
the *England-woz-great-before-you-got-ere* speech
came frothing from his chipped lip while I stood
dumb, counting on the usual passive stance
that had worked so well in previous conflicts.
But no, the stream of abuse was endless.
Your dad's fish smells worse than yer mother's cunt!
I had no choice. I would have to summon up
the eloquence of the layman, that
backs-to-the-wall mentality they so loved.

'Listen,' I said. 'My dad makes the best
chips in Loughton. Proper English ones too,
not the poncey crap you get down the road.'
That's the spirit. You tell im. More laughter.
Ah. So you got yer tongue back then ay, chink.
Well, tell me then, part from yer fish and chips,
what have you dog-eating scum given us?
'Well, we pay our taxes, we create jobs,
give you something to eat before midnight.'
My voice, startled, grew louder with confidence.

Yeah well, apart from that, he said tersely –
'and tea, gunpowder, chow mein, soya sauce,
kung fu movies,' I said, interrupting.
'China keeps the economy going.
Those sweatshop workers keep the prices down.
Where do you think that England shirt was made?
That white label there says Made in China!'
The bar turned silent, stunned. An equaliser.
Good build-up play from the opposition
had led to that glorious opening.

So. Half-time and things were finely balanced.
Pints would be refilled, commentaries resumed
(after the break – someone's bowels were bursting)
and when the whistle blew the game exploded
into action again. 'Come on England,'
I said. *You betta keep yer trap shut
or I'm gonna carve yer fuckin face up,*
said the skinhead, facing the impatient crowd.
This cunt's takin the piss, the fuckin chink,
which prompted this slew of responses:

*Psst. His mum's English. Through and through. He's got
the crown on his passport. He ain't Chinese.
He's Malaysian. All look the same to me.
I don't care what he looks like, what matters
is where his loyalties lie.* Heads nodded.
Tebbit's law had just ruled in my favour!
*Just coz this cunt has a passport don't mean
he earnt the right to be ere,* sneered our skin,
the fucker's takin us for a free ride.
At this he leaked his pint across a table.

'Bollocks. I've as much right to this place as you,'
I said. 'My granddad was a Desert Rat.
7th Armoured Division. They pushed Rommel
from Egypt. And my other granddad helped
with the Jap Resistance in Borneo.
That's fighting on two continents for you.
What did your old man do during the war?'
Beer mats puffed up with the spirit of yesteryear,
Spitfire, London Pride, good old English ale,
mopping up the stains from his awkward spill.

Yer talkin out yer arse. What fuckin war?
Incredulous murmurs in the background.
We ain't fought you cunts since we took Hong Kong.
Groans. That last shot was well wide of its mark.
Shoulda dropped the bomb on you cockroaches,
he laughed, visibly discomfited, knowing
he had erred, then tried to switch topic.
An don't talk bout me fuckin old man, he's
dead and gone, left me only with ma pride.
Ain't none of you gonna take that from me.

Quieter now, as though exhaustion had caught up,
the skin leant close to me with his beer breath.
Alrite, yer makin me miss the match.
Just tell me, are yer with me or against me?
(as if there was any doubt in my answer).
'How many times do I have to say this.
I came here to support the En-ger-land
and sing along just like the rest of you.'
His squinted eyes lightened. *That's alright then.*
He hobbled his way back across the floor.

My acceptance finalised, victory
assured, I left before the match finished.
A crisis averted, I could not tell
whether England's joint efforts would be enough
to see them battle through these testing times.
Outside was the beginning of a riot,
St. George's pennants were ablaze everywhere.
I felt a growling impetus inside me
as I made my turn, a half-baked Englishman,
watching the sign clatter and swing from its post.
My *Three Lions Pub*, its pride not dimmed at all.

THE NATIONAL FLAG

All the national papers announced it:
a new flag to represent the diverse
background of the kingdom's loyal subjects,
pride of place next to the royal standard
and the gratitude of the whole nation
for the competition's winning entry.

Though knowing where to start can be tricky –
finding out what rules a flag must observe,
whatever holds the centre together;
a cross, a crescent, a six-pointed star,
yin and yang, spots, stripes, circles, a rhombus,
something the schoolchildren will remember.

So, what to include? Colours, insignias,
a tricolour, a hammer and sickle,
perhaps a pithy motto or emblem,
some small 'unity in diversity'
arranged between tinctures of various shade
or divided up by a strip or band.

Next, the symbolic colours: red for blood,
green for land, blue, the far flung horizons
and black, the might of a united race.
But be wary of a flag that wants more
than it can hold onto, or much worse,
one that is mistaken for another.

Maybe, if I could have it all my way,
I'd capture the earth's singularity
and sketch the constellations while I move,
knowing then I'd contain all multitudes –
each bright star, infinite, ungraspable,
touching lightly on an empty canvas.

HOME, ON THE RUN

Once, I went on the run thinking
I'd escape from all this madness.
My rucksack was duffed and dirtied
through years of service and schooling,
worn-through and dull wintered
in the locker of my mind.

Latched together like so many scars,
its rips and folds held me gingerly
while a dozen panels zipped up the times
I had outlived in nervous urgency.
Held up like an immense weight,
it was impossible to put back down again.

I had it strapped against my heart
and was sure there'd be no turning back.
That first step was all I needed –
momentum alone would drive me forward
out of doors, past familiar signs,
to the station – onward journey, no return.

But, sitting down, I pull out my notes,
my jumble of clothes, and what
do I find but home spilling out
of this backpack, pile upon pile
of life's essential memories
tumbling heedless from its sack.

You can't escape the things you carry with you.
Either I must strip my body raw
to the bone, cleave myself out of sight
or learn to love this state of exile,
like these teenage fictions I lose myself in daily,
illuminated, exposed on the run.

MUTANT

HOME ON THE RUN

Forged by the world but not of it,
I am that most composite of creatures:
your hybrid monster, chimera
whose progeny you never planned.

Away from your pregnant furnace
I clang and grip for a second birth.
My misshapen figure lies heavy against
the metallic faces of this earth.

My heat was borne on human hands.
Now, my blood will darken and congeal
in embers of desire, then spill,
as love does, across distant lands.

I am nowhere. I am everywhere.
No island is out of reach, no shore too distant.
My every breath will slay the horizons.
Airborne, I weld myself into arcs of light,

split the sun's baptismal rays
into rainbows. My prismatic gaze
has set the world apart and dispersed
the teeming multitudes.

Resurrected daily,
I stand poised above fields, casting
myself over borders whose shadows
flee with their armies into the night.

I have spent an eternity in your myths,
always a brief step from home.
I wave at that unknown tribe on the margin,
shaking loose my ancestors' limbs.

No earth I inherit will take me back
into its furnace now. Out of my one sun
will come a thousand burnished blades.
Each child will singe within my flames.

SPEED DATING

Let's pretend this is not a game:
you and I mean well and intend
to make a go of it, though we tell
our friends it's nothing serious,
and joke of strange and bungled matches
with misfits and dark-eyed fanatics
whose antics speak of shallow breeding
and casual hints on one-night stands.

But let's turn now to the issues at hand –
how our lonely hearts trudge on ahead
in a loser's parade, blacked out in ink,
how talk ends abruptly on a spur
when we decline the subject of money
or small-talk to compare blood types
and signs, with our thoughts eclipsing
as we jettison our dreams each time.

Forgive my being earnest here,
but ever since you sat down with me
something has been happening to us,
something beautiful and unspoken,
a brief span of our lives in miniature
no less, as our fingertips brush slyly
and we lean forward trading looks
that candles make desirable.

It might not seem obvious to you,
but I see with each candid answer
and the hope writ across your palms
that we are soulmates of a kind
so before we part our restless ways

I've been meaning to ask you this
simple question – whether you might
say yes if I asked you to marry me?

CROSSINGS

1 THE GREAT STEPPE

B.C. 20,000

This levelling plain beckoned early man
en route to that first crossing,
harried him to the very edge
and carried his first seed along the wind,
planted him in different corners
but tore his roots from under him
and kept him immured, silent,
preserved in a cavern of bones,
a mongrel's treasure horde.

The years pass, the snow thaws,
the glacial passage eases its resolve.
Those lost souls bent low from the hunt
and the voyage across frozen time
now creep back up to the surface.
They want to know who made it,
who survived the gauntlet
of ice across the frigid wastelands,
whose legacy multiplied with each footstep.

But no human sounds are heard here.
Only the muffled pad of snout
on grass preys on their loneliness.
Those whose bones are flecks of millennia
prick their muddy ears out of rugged earth,
ready to snatch at the wind's murmur,
that jangle and jabber like a shaman's relic
waiting to be summoned by an ancient tongue
or the throaty hack of an axe or spade.

Surely someone will discover them.
Surely some new-found descendant will
inter them in hospitable times.
But no clan now will reclaim them
or pile them up high in concrete urns.
No nation will eulogise these strangers
or trade them a place in their epic tale.
They guided our progress but lie forgotten,
crushed under the weight of so much history.

2 MISSIONARIES

B.C. 400 – A.D. 700

They picked their way round mountains,
desert plains and caravan tracks,
through well-worn passages,
reciting omens, translating scriptures,
memorising the hard-won phrase.
No compromise would see them settle
for lesser treasure than human hearts,
no earthly burden would test their mettle.
Theirs was a mission with no end.

One group sought the middle way,
an escape from life by embracing life;
Awakened Ones, princes who dethroned
their material ambition and came
to answer the call of an Emperor
who saw a man burnished all in gold
and held the sun and moon in thrall.
They would leave their knees sunk as
solidly as stone and need never be reborn.

Another lot brought salvation with them
to fulfil the work of their anointed one,
combining their faith within their spirits
to prove that the human and divine
remained mingled, united in one.
Luminous, consecrated, steeple-bound,
their heads raging with Messianic flame,
their forbearance would see the world
prepare for the coming revelation.

And still there came upon the wind voices
that called the people to heed the command
of the one and only, whose sacred book
would restore his uncorrupted words.
Through time and history they come
roaming the sands against heresy,
replacing the blood of conquest
with the ink of the reasoned scholar,
submitting themselves to the will of God.

What prophecies they would all foretell,
each missionary vying with the rest
to stake their hold on these crossroads of fate,
stretching their faith far across the world.

3 REFUGEES

A.D. 376

Sudden they came, like frost in the long night,
stalking the forked paths of birds in winter
and spilling out of fir and pine heartlands
to lead their flock from darkness and famine.
The weary sentries could not hold them back,
rivers diverted their mouths to feed them.
Bands of men, their sick wives and crude offspring
rushed over dykes and palisades in rags
pleading, *please, let us serve in your Empire.*

Goaded and chased by a feral impulse,
they came rushing through swathes of dry grassland
to be transplanted like tiny seedlings,
scattered over fields to rise prickly blades
that fought back in scorn the scourge that first threshed
their kin and whittled them down, like ripe corn.
Guttural were their cries, hard their living;
they knew no rest, no respite from old wounds,
feeling the conflict of stones drawing roads
under their feet, telling them where to go.

They learnt to wield a new tongue from their hoes,
servile to villas and estates, working
as farmers, craftsmen, runners and soldiers,
sweating under a Roman sun whose flame
they would one day inherit, whose zenith
would stare the world down. A tribal nation,
they will mould themselves onto their old hosts
and crown themselves as princes of the land,
sending their brass arms over the field's edge,
ready to repulse the next foreign band.

4 HORSE-HEAD FIDDLE

A.D. 1000

I have gathered from my fallen steed
his dreams
and woven them onto his body again.

He came to me and reared
his muzzled head,
then beckoned me to his grave,

told me to pluck my sorrow
from his bones
and fold his ribs over an empty heart,

store his voiceless echo inside
a hollow box
and wrap his sturdy hide around it.

Gathered up between my thighs again,
we ride in unison
as his bridle quickens beneath my hands.

His neck will steady the vibrations
as his tail catches the wind
and the bow slants in my hand.

Together we'll harness our forces,
rein in those songs
then gallop through the rhythms.

Ride always with your spirit in my veins,
free and unrestrained.
You will never be alone again.

5 SUBOTAI

A.D. 1245

I have pitched my tent on all four corners
of the steppes, led my faithful horde to war,
criss-crossed the frozen rivers to pillage
and set the enemy's lives in motion.

It was there for the taking, an open
expanse poised for our greed and harrowing,
stooped too low to refuse our raider's jaws.
The skies circled above us wherever we went.

We sent the ground tumbling beneath our hooves
and stormed from the wilderness of our birth,
washed away cities to restore the lie
of the land, absorb the riches of the earth.

No city could repulse our eager thrusts.
No maid's churlish look soured our appetite.
Far from home, we hoarded the grassland
and swelled the Altai steppes with wolfish cries.

But the cubs scrapped over their father's bones,
tore his legacy apart limb by limb
and set his pack to flight across the world,
staining their fur pelts with their kin's own blood.

Our tracks yielded to roads clogged with carts
of Chinese silk, Persian spices, then we fell
to bargaining with coin, not iron, abandoned
our nomad ways for the comfort of cities.

I am Subotai, last of the war hounds,
once commander of all that I surveyed.
I see with one eye the dread cheaply bought,
the galloping hordes crush the lightning stares.

Here I stand, astride my broken chariot,
a spent pack-horse crippled by uncertainty
among the rabble of my liege lord's heirs.
A lone cry scours the sky for you my lord.

I would have seized the reins of war for you,
sprung the vision of peace beneath our rule,
let loose the chains that shackle our story
so all would know the burden of our glory.

6 IL MILIONE

A.D. 1295

No one knew or cared when I resurfaced
with breathless tales of wonder from the East,
that I had sunk and was borne in earnest
by the truth of currents that would release
me back into my homestead. They knew not
where this stranger had come from or what goods
he bartered in distant lands, what he sought
when he knocked on the doors of relatives
and cried dismally in their lifeless arms.

And what a treasure trove I had brought back,
as I showed them all on that fateful night;
not only silk, or jade or porcelain –
these steadied hands but not eyes from the sight
of China shapes kept in clear proportion,
swathed in a culture as fine as our own,
drafted in oils and summoned forth by lines
of characters liberated from time.

Parched dry and blinded by systems of change,
they knew not from what reason to contend
sound proof of my tale which they found so strange,
and so I wrote a book that would defend
my trials and tribulations with this pen.
Not multi-headed beasts or crimson seas,
we'd find horizons rotating again,
to shift the world inch by inch in degrees.

But my friends picked it up, cross-referenced
my figures to the statute of the Cross,
scribbled corrections and censored whole lines,

traded in words that were no longer mine.
If they could just see things the way I did,
they would have known better than to disguise
true history from the riches that it hides.

Whatever they said about my travels,
know this: nothing can take away the fact
I was that blessed one in a million
who marvelled at God's creations with pride
and crossed that wide gulf to bridge their divide.

7 THE GREAT WALL

A.D. 1644–

Walls, where the fissure
of history opens its gap
to garrison my present thinking

as I stand on ramparts
surveying the contours
of a thousand years of struggle,

the ground still raw
where a kingdom drew its line,
the contest still unwon.

One celestial son made his mark here,
his patchwork of forts
interred with those that built them,

a task as brazen as the banners
that came to conquer it,
and what is left

but rotten corpses
that churn the gut of fields,
fertilised anew among weeds?

A repeating flashback:
whether by treachery or force
the idle core was shaken,

another crumbling mandate,
a return to parsimony,
an exchange of names and seals,

so why bother
to furrow the earth
and rise up such pretensions?

Maybe I should learn
from my own divided state
to settle such contradictions,

construct turrets of my own
and buttress human nature
with my own habitations,

brood among these cold stones
and contemplate
like an unwilling guard

that unsettling twilight
drawing nearer and nearer
with the desert sands –

just as these plaintive trees
decry their duty in
holding back the frontier.

Swung into rank formation,
they monitor the horizon
with their girdled branches,

criss-cross one another,
their simple lives forced
again, into unnatural walls.

DRAGONS RISING

They come flying across azure skies,
straddling great earthenware hills,
paddling out of sunken depths
and rousing eyelids from stumps of trees.
Like great rivers, their torsos writhe and coil
at every bend. Under each crevice,
beside each faint shadow, they emerge
from all the elements to speak to me.

The greatest amongst them are flanked by
crab-nosed guards from brittle glass palaces
who will order me to pay them homage
with my hornless head hung low
and my claws sheathed and bowed.
I must pray for their benevolence,
always obedient, never pleading
for them to turn their gaze from me.

They will hold me fast in their embrace
like a prodigal son newly returned,
whisper at origins beyond the Eastern seas
and lash their tails across great continents,
eager to measure their momentous tides
with their old-age wisdom and their charm,
expecting to see their offspring running
back in droves before their immortal eyes.

They tell me I too can pass through
this arched gateway to heavenly peace,
that my scales will glisten with pride again.
Spewing up great mouthfuls of smoke,
they tell me everything has changed.

You are descended from dragons
they say, stretching their gleaming talons
behind their backs. You belong to us now.

ARRIVALS

I think of all the places I have been,
where the restless hours have taken me,
hurling my lamp and my fire across distant lands
only to pick my way through burning ground
and stumble blindly through visions
ransomed to the few by the many.
I held myself hostage to the impulse of others:
now I must wrestle habit's stubborn strand
and unwind my thought's confining bands
to bid the blood flow back to my limbs.

And now, as the sun wheels like a compass
and the world turns sudden from its axis
to cast its burden upon my back,
now that my routes have fallen all around me,
I must go back to the very beginning.
Back, where my past folds out and spreads before me
as one complete life, where events flow and mingle
with the great little lies the world revolves around.
Now I must lead the tongue's forked path onward
to find it passing on through forever.

Though friends shall comb the rugged hills for me
I will have gone far out to a place they cannot follow,
wandering once more on that crowded shore,
a refugee of my own drowned desire.
I contemplate again that first journey
like the lost heroic tempers of old,
thinking that, after the hourglass drops
and darkness creeps over my footsteps,

when all time stands still with me as I survey this,
my blighted kingdom, alone, unfostered, outspoken,
I too can say that I have made my landing.

I too can say that I have finally arrived.

ACKNOWLEDGEMENTS

Grateful acknowledgements are due to the editors of the following journals and anthologies where some of these poems first appeared: *Acumen: A Literary Journal, Asia Literary Review, Cha: An Asian Literary Journal, Envoi, Quarterly Literary Review Singapore, The Best New British and Irish Poets 2016*.

A number of these poems have been performed over the years for the Hong Kong International Literary Festival (2008-2012), while an earlier draft of the collection was a finalist for the HKU Poetry Prize (2010) and highly commended for The Melita Hume Prize (2012). The poem '45 Belgrave Square' was nominated by *Cha* for a Pushcart Prize in 2010.

I am grateful to Todd Swift, Director of Eyewear Publishing, for his support and encouragement, and to Alex Wylie for his wise and patient editing of the collection. My thanks also to Shirley Geok-lin Lim and Tim Dooley for their kind words in the blurbs, and to Vahni Capildeo and Louise Ho for their judges' comments on the manuscript. Finally, my thanks to Edwin Smet, for the gorgeous cover design, and to Aaron T Michelson, who takes a mean photo.

I am indebted to a number of people who have encouraged, goaded and challenged my writing over the years: in particular Reid Mitchell, Andrew Barker, Tammy Ho Lai-Ming, Rosie McLaughlin, Akin Jeje, David McKirdy and Sam Powney. Thanks also to my friends, rogues, companions who make up the Peel Street Poetry Collective and Poetry OutLoud HK. You are like a second family to me. Finally, none of this would be possible without the love and support of my family whose personal journeys and migrations echo throughout this work, and especially to my beloved wife Anna and son Jasper, who must bear the cost of living with my art. I love you all.